D1283728

TULSA TIMES
A PICTORIAL HISTORY:
THE BOOM YEARS

Photographs From the Beryl D. Ford Collection

Text by Susan Everly-Douze
Edited by Terrell Lester

Copyright © 1987 by
World Publishing Co.
318 S. Main Mall / P.O. Box 1770
Tulsa, Okla., 74102

ISBN: 0-941093-02-6

All rights reserved. No part of this book may be
reproduced without the prior written permission
of the publisher.

Printed by Western Printing Company, Inc.
Tulsa, Oklahoma

FOREWORD

The way we were in pictures. That's again the focus of "Tulsa Times: A Pictorial History."

Volume II portrays "The Boom Years: 1912 to 1942." Tulsa launched itself into those three decades not only by shedding its cow-town image for good but also by proclaiming itself Oil Capital of the World.

The camera's eye was there when the skyscrapers that oil dollars built began to stud city blocks, constantly revising the skyline. It recorded new bridges, new rail and bus terminals, new refineries, new department stores and miles of freshly paved roads that stretched into new neighborhoods where cows not long ago grazed.

When Tulsa reveled in a barnstorming fly-in visit from Charles Lindbergh and resolved to become an aviation center, the camera looked skyward to record the city's progress.

Growing pains, as well as Tulsa's proud moments, also were put into focus. The camera no longer was just in the hands of professional lensmen who came to town to pose merchants in front of their stores or millionaires in their mansions. When Tulsa was wracked by a race riot, swept by flood waters and crippled by the Depression, there were snapshots from amateurs to preserve the tragedies.

From formal portraits to the snapshots, "Tulsa Times" presents a photographic collage of the 30 years of the city's most extraordinary growth. The majority of the pictures once again comes from the Beryl D. Ford Collection, undoubtedly the most extensive assembly of Tulsa photo memorabilia.

Ford's enthusiasm for preserving Tulsa's past in pictures only is excelled by his command of the city's history. This knowledge was invaluable in annotating the picture book.

Russell Gideon, the Tulsa World's in-house historian, merits a special thanks.

TABLE OF CONTENTS

The year was 1916. The Model T virtually had replaced the horse and buggy and Tulsa was on the rise with new skyscraper construction. The Hunt Building, later the home of the Brown-Dunkin department store, would be built on the construction site in the foreground, Fourth and Main streets.

BOOM TOWN

At the century's turn, Tulsa's skyline was diminutive — mostly crude homes and hastily constructed stores clustered around the Frisco Railroad tracks. Cattle drives took over the unpaved streets.

But the 1905 discovery of the nearby Glenn Pool, the richest oil field the world had yet to see, stirred the sleepy cow town. The gushers were across the river, but Tulsans were determined to make their town the center of oil action.

To house what they brazenly dubbed the "Oil Capital of the World" would require office buildings and municipal facilities, hotels and banks. And in 1912, Tulsa kicked off a building boom that would last for two decades.

Land prices soared as skyscrapers began to sprout like derricks. Fortunes were made in real estate as easily as in black gold, and every oil magnate, from W.G. Skelly to Josh Cosden, seemed to have a building with his name on it. By the '20s, the Chamber of Commerce had 50 millionaires on its finance committee, said to be the greatest assemblage of wealth to serve a civic board in the country.

Brick plants were working overtime.

By 1912, there was a stately courthouse; by 1917, a federal building that gave the post office its first permanent home.

Cosden, Tulsa's so-called "Prince of Petroleum," pierced the skyline with the city's first true skyscraper. His 14-story building, 409 S. Boston Ave., was completed in 1918.

Banks, the lifeblood of the speculative oil industry, also became a prominent part of the cityscape. The Exchange National Bank, founded in 1910 specifically to meet the needs of oilmen, developed a national reputation as "the oil bank." By 1929, the bank had stretched its soaring 28-story headquarters over an entire block of Boston Avenue between Third and Fourth streets. The bank became the National Bank of Tulsa, and ultimately, the Bank of Oklahoma.

By 1930, city boosters bragged that Tulsa stood "twelfth in the number of tall buildings in all America." There were 37 buildings of 10 to 20 stories each and two at 20-plus.

Fortune-making was not, however, confined to offices and banks. In fact, the Tulsa buildings that probably put a roof over most oil deals were the hotels. First the Hotel Tulsa, then the Mayo were stately on the outside, but their lobbies constantly were awhirl with armchair drilling. It was a cast of characters that continued to grow. By the '30s, hundreds of oil companies and the firms that supplied them called Tulsa home. The uncanny foresight of a town with not a drop of its own, but that would be Oil Capital, had worked.

Tulsa in 1913, looking north, with the courthouse at Sixth Street and Boulder Avenue in the foreground.

Tulsa in 1915, looking north on Boston Avenue at Fourth Street, with the Kennedy Building under construction and the YMCA at the right.

Main Street, looking south toward Third Street in 1917.

Looking north on Main Street from Third Street about 1924.

Third Street and Boston Avenue in the mid-'20s.

In the mid-'20s, snow-covered streets were shoveled by hand. *Top right,* Fifth Street looking east across Boulder Avenue. *Right,* Fifth Street and Boston Avenue.

The original Tulsa County Courthouse, 521 S. Boulder Ave., was completed in 1912.

In the early teens, residences dominated the northwest corner of Third Street and Boulder Avenue.

By 1916, on the same corner, the homes were gone and construction of Tulsa's first federal building-post office was in full swing.

The facility was ready for business in July 1917. Until then, the post office had depended upon rented downtown space.

Despite the Depression, Tulsa launched the '30s by expanding the white stone structure along the entire block and adding a third floor.

Arkansas river from the
Philtower – Cosden refinery
in background – Tulsa, Okla.
1274-1

PAUL STITHEM
TULSA

The Mayo Hotel punctuated the 1927 skyline, with the Cosden refinery in the background.

17

Tulsa in 1928, looking south along Cheyenne Avenue at Second Street. The Exchange National Bank was being topped out to dwarf the once prominent Philtower building. The Mayo Hotel was at the right.

Looking north on Main Street from Second Street in 1930.

In 1932, Mecca Coffee Co. called 209 S. Boulder Ave. home.

The Tulsa World building, on the east side of Boulder Avenue between Third and Fourth streets, in 1935. Wieners at the Coney Island Sandwich Shop next door were 5 cents each.

As Tulsa grew, homes, many soon to be demolished, coexisted with skyscrapers. This was the site of the current YMCA on the east side of Denver Avenue between Fifth and Sixth streets. The Mayo Hotel, completed in 1925, was in the left background.

Best illustrating Tulsa's building boom was the site of Producers National Bank, just west of Main Street on Third Street. This was the bank in 1927, but the site already had been occupied earlier in the century by the two-story Tulsa World building that also housed the United States Court. By 1930, S.H. Kress & Co. took over and built a six-story addition. The Kress Building was demolished in 1974 to make way for development of the Williams Center.

A Depression-era project, the Warehouse Market, 11th Street and Elgin Avenue, was built on the site of the old McNulty ball park. Originally called the Public Market, it was Tulsa's biggest grocery store, but in its early days still sold chickens live to customers who waited as their bird of choice was killed and cleaned. *Below*, the market when it opened; *right*, the market in 1942; *below right*, the market's cafe on the west end of the building.

Downtown Tulsa in 1932.

23

24   The downtown skyline from the northwest in 1940.

Looking north across Sixth and Main streets about 1942.

The First National Bank of Tulsa, on the northwest corner of Second and Main streets, *above*, in 1912, was the successor to the city's first bank, the Tulsa Banking Co., and catered to would-be oil barons. The building boasted the city's first elevator. *Left*, the bank's new home on the northeast corner of Fourth and Main streets in 1918.

Tulsa banks, the lifeblood of the speculative oil business, grew as fast as the city's skyline. The Clinton Building, *left*, went up on the northwest corner of Fourth Street and Boston Avenue in 1913 only to be razed in 1928 for the new headquarters of the Exchange National Bank, *below*, established in 1910 to meet the needs of oilmen. *Far left*, in 1929, the finished product stretched from Third to Fourth streets. The bank later became the National Bank of Tulsa and, ultimately, the Bank of Oklahoma.

Completed by the Mayo brothers in 1925, the Mayo Hotel, *right*, on the northeast corner of Fifth Street and Cheyenne Avenue, would replace the Hotel Tulsa as the city's premier hostelry both for "armchair drilling" and entertaining. *Above*, the lobby where dinner was advertised for $1.50.

The Mincks Hotel, 403 S. Cheyenne Ave., was completed in the '20s by Isaiah S. "Ike" Mincks. The richly ornate, rococo structure became the Adams Hotel and a Tulsa landmark as the city's finest example of terra cotta ornamentation. Mincks lost the hotel during the Depression. *Right*, the Mincks coffee shop.

The Almore Apartments, 1300 block of South Peoria Avenue, in 1928, and the Annex Hotel, northeast corner of Third Street and Cincinnati Avenue, in the '30s.

The Hotel Tulsa, at the northwest corner of Third Street and Cincinnati Avenue, opened in 1912, and its lobby quickly became headquarters for the biggest of oil boom deals. Everyone, including oil barons J. Paul Getty, Harry Sinclair and Josh Cosden, came with maps in hand and deals were sealed with a handshake.

From pioneer landmark to eyesore by 1942, the Brady Hotel, at Archer and Main streets, was the most popular hotel in early Tulsa and headquarters for early Democratic politics. The Brady lost its clout, however, as the city moved south. One of the city's most spectacular fires in 1935 sealed its fate as a hostelry.

The Alvin Hotel, at Seventh and Main streets, was built in 1928. The hotel's grandest claim to fame was being the birthplace in April 1938 of the Society for the Preservation of Barbershop Quartet Singing in America. The Alvin balcony overlooked Seventh Street.

32　　Elegance was standard in both the Alvin Hotel's lobby, *above*, and coffee shop, *opposite page*.

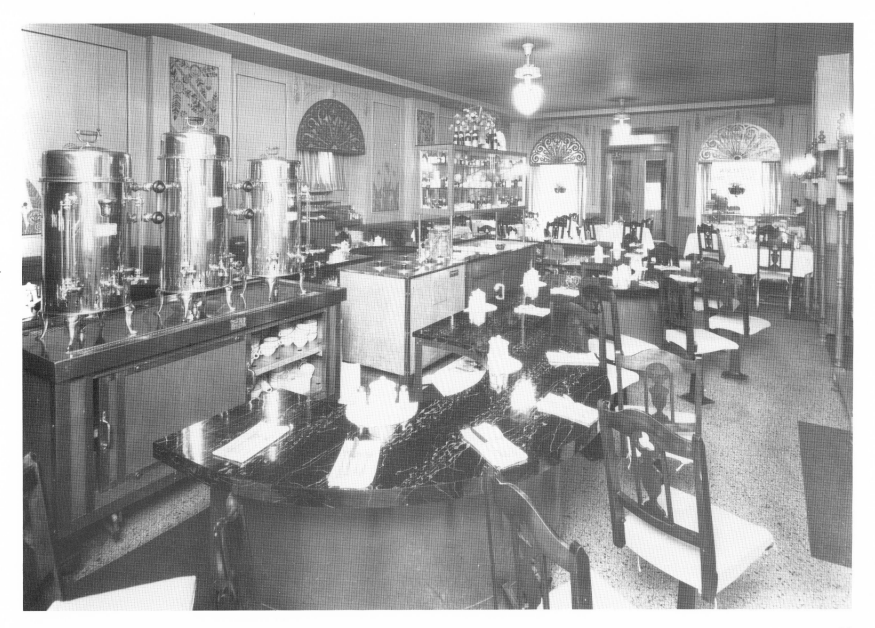

Tulsa's downtown skyscrapers in 1940 provided a backdrop for the D-X refinery's field of tanks across the Arkansas River in West Tulsa.

OIL CAPITAL OF THE WORLD

In 1923, oilman Earl P. Harwell built a 30-room Tudor mansion on a scenic bluff overlooking the Arkansas River. For the mansion dwellers, the Arkansas was a buffer against the oil refineries smoking away on its west bank.

Not far away, spanking-new skyscrapers offered up the same river-refinery view.

Mansions. Skyscrapers. The panorama of refineries neatly confined to the west side of the river. All were pieces of the dazzling picture that posed Tulsa as "Oil Capital of the World."

The claim could have been considered boastful. Tulsa had no oil wells of its own — in fact, wouldn't even allow a gusher to be drilled in the city limits. There were other towns closer to the lush Mid-Continent oil fields. But early on, Tulsa decided it would be more than a boom town; it would be a business center providing oilmen with hotels and homes, banks and office space.

The strategy worked.

"Armchair drilling" in the lobbies of Tulsa hotels, sealed with a handshake, resulted in more deals than were consummated in the fields. The opening of the Hotel Tulsa in 1912 came the same year as the discovery of the Cushing field. More than a billion dollars was said to have changed hands in the hotel over 15 years — including Josh Cosden's famous $15 million check.

By 1915, the Chamber of Commerce publication Tulsa Spirit proclaimed that "one-half of the coal, oil and gasoline consumed throughout the entire world comes from the district of which Tulsa is the center."

Although Tulsa said "no" to wells on its home front, the city saw enough dollar signs to dirty its hands — but only on the *other* side of the river — with refineries. By 1910, five years after the discovery of the Glenn Pool, Texas Company, now Texaco, Inc., built its refinery in West Tulsa. Cosden followed a year later with a second plant that earned him personal millions and became the largest independent refinery in the world.

By 1940, the Chamber of Commerce was boasting 40 major oil companies plus 400 smaller companies and operators. That was not to mention hundreds more businesses and manufacturers that sprung up to cater to them.

Tulsa became the purchasing headquarters for the oil industry. By 1940, it was estimated that the oil companies headquartered in Tulsa annually purchased $300 million in oil supplies and equipment.

Their clout was particularly apparent in 1923 when oilman W.G. Skelly ramrodded the first International Petroleum Exposition. It would become one of the largest trade shows on earth, the world's fair of the oil industry. And for decades after, Tulsa's oilmen called the shots.

It was the oilmen, not their suppliers, who would decide when the next expo would be; and if the suppliers wanted to sell to these barons of the Oil Capital, they had better be there.

Workmen laying pipe in the prolific Glenn Pool that put Tulsa on the map as "Oil Capital of the World."

36   The Glenn Pool and nearby tank farms.

Carter Oil Co. workers unloading pipe.

The Texaco refinery filled West Tulsa's sky with smoke when 35,000 barrels of oil burned.

Employee housing in
the oil fields around Tulsa.

37

A major player in the Mid-Continent oil fields, Carter Oil Co., a subsidiary of Standard Oil Co. (N.J.), was founded by Col. John Carter of Titusville, Pa., in 1893. Tulsa became its general operating headquarters in 1915. *Below*, employee housing.

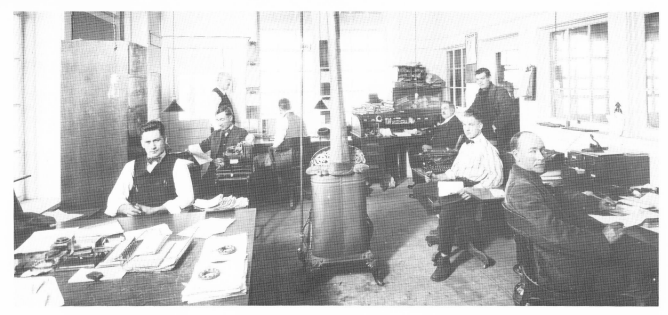

The Carter Oil Co.'s boiler shop and plant offices.

The D-X refinery, viewed from downtown in the '30s.

Derricks formed the gateway to an early International Petroleum Exposition which became one of the largest trade shows on earth, the world's fair of the oil industry.

41

The first IPE was staged in 1923 at the Convention Hall, now Brady Theater, 105 W. Brady St., and spilled onto roped-off streets. The IPE started as a "side-street machinery fair" with only 27 exhibits and an attendance of 14,203.

A parade of floats, complete with a King Petroleum and Queen Petrolia, gave the first IPE a carnival atmosphere. The brass band marched to the Convention Hall playing "Yes, We Have No Bananas."

By 1940, the IPE had mushroomed into 628 exhibits and an attendance of 194,491.

In 1927, the IPE established its permanency with the erection of buildings near the fairgrounds. Aviator Charles Lindbergh was a special guest and President Calvin Coolidge pressed a button in the White House that sent oil gushing at the Tulsa showgrounds. This is an artist's conception and an aerial view of the new facility surrounded by empty countryside.

43

As Tulsa's love affair with black gold and the automobile blossomed, oil companies responded with gasoline stations befitting the city's claim of "Oil Capital of the World." This was the Griffith-Bynum station, 13th Street and Boston Avenue.

The Penoco Oil Co. station, First Street and Frisco Avenue, featured not only gas pumps but also a cafe, barber shop and pool tables.

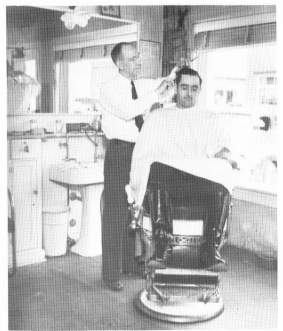

The Phillips Petroleum Co. station, 15th Street and Cincinnati Avenue, about 1925.

The Marland Refining Co. station on the northeast corner of Sixth Street and Peoria Avenue. The sign at the left read: "Yes sir, we'll gladly drain your crankcase."

A Phillips Petroleum Co. filling station, 2224 E. Admiral Blvd., about 1927.

A Mid-Continent Co. station, southwest corner of Fifth Street and Cincinnati Avenue, in 1928.

In 1937, Dutch Rogers' station offered a car wash for 50 cents and round-the-clock service. The taller pumps dispensed Phillips 77, an early premium fuel.

48

On Route 66 in the late '20s, the Pierce Pennant Terminal, 12200 E. 11th St., was Tulsa's earliest motel.

Cyrus Avery's Texaco station at the traffic circle, Admiral Place and Mingo Road, in the mid-'20s.

W.G. Skelly was considered "Mr. Tulsa," and the Skelly Building, Fourth Street and Boulder Avenue, was his headquarters.

The Philtower, 427 S. Boston Ave., was built by oilman Waite Phillips in 1928 at the cost of $2.5 million. The architect was Edward Delk, who also designed Phillips' home, now the Philbrook Art Museum.

Built in 1919, the Sinclair Building, Fifth and Main streets, was the original headquarters of the billion-dollar oil company founded by Harry F. Sinclair.

The McFarlin Building, 11 E. Fifth St., was built in 1918 by Robert M. McFarlin, co-founder of McMan Oil Co., and his nephew, James Chapman.

The Cosden Building, 409 S. Boston Ave., was completed in 1918. At 14 stories, it was considered Tulsa's first skyscraper. Its first owner was Josh Cosden, dubbed the Prince of Petroleum and the Rubberball of the Petroleum Industry because he made and lost two fortunes. Today, the structure is called the Mid-Continent Building.

51

Owning a commanding view of West Tulsa refineries, the 30-room English Tudor mansion of E.P. Harwell, 2210 S. Main St., was built in 1923. It became Harwelden, home to the Arts and Humanities Council.

The J.M. Gillette Mansion, 15th Street and Yorktown Place, was built in 1921 by businessman James Max Gillette as his "country place." Pure-bred cattle grazed in the backyard of the Gothic Tudor retreat.

Built in 1918, the Skelly Mansion, 21st Street and Madison Avenue, was as grand as the man who built it. W.G. Skelly, *right*, made his fortune in gushers then went on to assure Tulsa's prominence in the aviation age.

E.W. Sinclair, *left*, president of Sinclair Refining Co. and brother of Harry Sinclair, president of Sinclair Consolidated Oil Co., was one of Tulsa's oil barons who helped assure the city's claim as "Oil Capital." His 25-room mansion was at 1730 S. Cheyenne Ave. He also became president of the Exchange National Bank, "the oilman's bank."

Philbrook, an Italian Renaissance-style villa designed by architect Edward Delk, was the home of oilman and philanthropist Waite Phillips. Completed in 1928, the mansion was donated as an art center in 1939. Today, it is the Philbrook Museum of Art. (*Courtesy of Philbrook*).

Philbrook's great hall.

Genevieve Phillips' bedroom.

A farm occupied the acreage before mansion construction began.

Waite Phillips

55

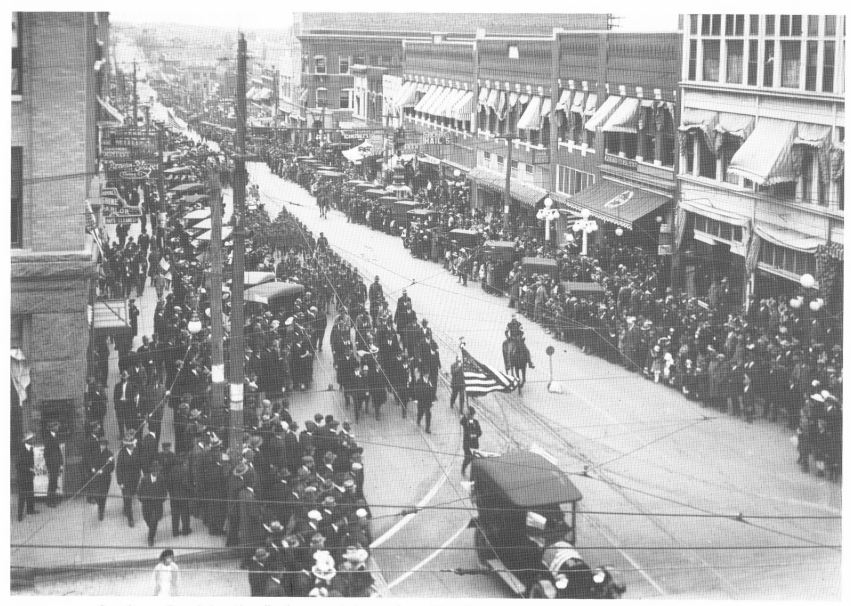

Crowds overflowed the sidewalks for a patriotic parade on Main Street in support of President Woodrow Wilson's call for a declaration of war in April 1917.

WAR AND THE HOME FRONT

The year was 1917, and the United States entered World War I. Tulsa rallied to the challenge with rousing home-front patriotism and, more importantly, an extra gush of black gold to grease the war machine.

The early war effort was desperate for petroleum. Tulsa-based oil companies responded by increasing their output by 25 percent. Oklahoma, as a result, was the country's leading oil-producing state for the war.

Tulsans also saw some of the initial action on the European Front. The Tulsa Ambulance Co. began its training at makeshift "Camp Sinclair" at the old Tulsa fairgrounds, Lewis Avenue and Archer Street, but still was selected to go to France first as part of the famed Rainbow Division.

After sending their sons to war, Tulsans got busy at home. The intersection of Fourth and Main streets was christened "Liberty Square" and became the headquarters of the Tulsa County Council of Defense. The group coordinated every civilian defense activity from bandage-making to tracking down draft dodgers and "liberty bond slackards," the latter, a serious faux pas to say the least, in a city that consistently bested its quota. A reward of $50 was paid for rounding up each draft dodger.

Men were mustered for the Tulsa County Home Guard to protect local oil fields and refineries and walk night patrols. Women produced more than a million surgical dressings and garnered pledges for food conservation. Companies volunteered employees' time for war activities. Young ladies did their part as hostesses for Tulsa's nationally famous Red Cross Canteen, near the Frisco Railroad station, where more than 15,000 soldiers in transit were met with ice tea and ice cream and provided with meals, emergency clothing and cigarettes.

Despite its oil-boom economy, Tulsa also felt the shortages of war. There were "Wheatless Wednesdays" and "Lightless Mondays" to conserve resources for the war front.

To keep spirits high, and raise war funds in the process, a "stunts committee" offered up wartime gambling games, including a roulette wheel spun for $1 to win $50 and $100 liberty bonds. Parades were routine patriotic fare and a giant flag was marched along Main Street for office workers to toss coins into.

Most heart-warming was the Victory Chorus, massive downtown community sings that drew 20,000 Tulsans to sing patriotic songs. "The Star-Spangled Banner" and "Old Folks at Home" were the favorites and could be heard a mile away.

When boys returned home, the city responded typically, erecting a huge arch, a replica of the Arc de Triomphe in Paris. Tulsans called it the Arch of Welcome.

Company C was Tulsa's original military unit, called up and mobilized overnight when trouble threatened on the Mexican border in 1916. Recalled to action for World War I, the company joined the 142nd Infantry, 36th Division in France. Many Tulsans were killed or wounded there.

The headquarters for the Tulsa County Council of National Defense, *right*, on Main Street between Fourth and Fifth streets. The council, one of thousands nationwide, coordinated war efforts on the home-front, including tracking down "liberty bond slackers." The War Savings Stamp Bank next door sold war stamps which patriotic Tulsans bought in record numbers.

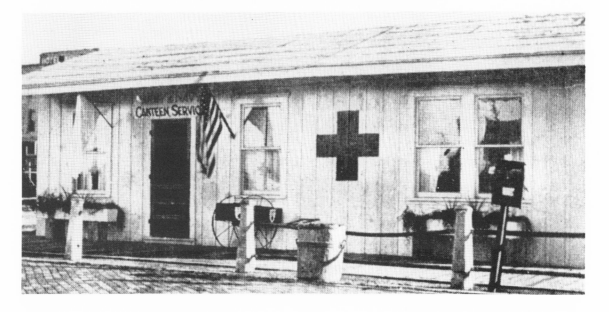

Thousands of soldiers were fed and cared for at the Tulsa Red Cross Canteen near the Frisco Railroad Depot. Red Cross activities dominated war-time Tulsa with women providing more than one million surgical bandages and companies routinely donating hours of their employees' time.

The Tulsa Ambulance Co. left from Camp Mills, N.Y., for France in 1917 where it joined the Rainbow Division. The company included almost the entire football team of Kendall College, now the University of Tulsa. Earlier training was at makeshift Camp Sinclair, named for oilman E.W. Sinclair, at the Tulsa Fairgrounds. Sinclair donated $10,000 to make the camp buildings more livable.

The Tulsa Ambulance Co. was in Neuenahr, Germany, in January 1919 as part of the Army of Occupation.

White-uniformed Red Cross nurses stood out during one of numerous patriotic parades that stopped Main Street traffic and had viewers hanging out of windows and perching on roof tops.

A blimp advertising war bonds glided over the Tulsa skyline in 1918. Looking south down Cincinnati Avenue from Standpipe Hill.

Tulsans depended on parades to keep home-front morale high.

An electric car bedecked with Confederate flags drew parade-goers' attention.

An Arch of Welcome was erected on Main Street between Third and Fourth streets to welcome home Company D, 111th Engineers. The arch, paid for by patriotic contributions, cost $3,500.

65

By 1929, downtown Tulsa could claim all the urban necessities — including packed parking lots. Parking cost 10 cents an hour. This was Sixth Street and Boston Avenue, looking northwest.

COMING OF AGE

Oil and water don't mix, but for Tulsa, the combination was an elixir to assure the city's continued prosperity.

By the '20s, Tulsa was awash with oil profits, confident with its self-proclaimed title of "Oil Capital of the World." Savvy oilmen realized, however, that their boom easily could bust because Tulsa was thirsty.

The city's main water supply was the Arkansas River, silty, brackish and increasingly polluted by oil refineries. Most Tulsans wouldn't drink it. Oilman Charles Page provided a temporary solution with his Sand Springs Bottled Water Co., which delivered five-gallon jugs to doorsteps daily.

How to wean Tulsa off the bottle produced the city's longest and probably most bitter civic battle. Page, already successful in the water business, argued that nearby Shell Creek Reservoir, that he had built for Sand Springs, also could quench Tulsa's thirst. His opponents envisioned a more impressive engineering feat, piping water, entirely by gravity flow, from Spavinaw Creek some 60 miles away. The $7.5 million Spavinaw plan won voters' support and one of the most daring engineering projects in the country at the time was under way.

Spavinaw water flowed into Tulsa taps in 1924 when President Calvin Coolidge pressed a telegraph key at the White House. The city celebrated with pageants, parades and street dancing and proclaimed its water the best in the nation.

Tulsa's growing pains, however, didn't evaporate with its new water supply.

Most signifcant, the railroad that gave birth to pioneer Tulsa was, by the '20s, competing for space with the increasingly popular automobile. As more trains pulled into Tulsa blocking intersections, massive traffic jams became routine. So did Tulsans' ire. As a result, the same year that Spavinaw water became reality, Tulsans found themselves voting for the second biggest civic project of the decade, the $3.5 million Union Depot that would become Tulsa's "New Front Door." Despite the Depression, ground was broken in November 1929.

The depot plan not only solved Tulsa's traffic problem with wide viaducts that carried four major downtown avenues over the tracks, but also maintained Tulsa's reputation as a railroad center.

The depot was heralded as the city's most magnificent improvement. The citizenry obviously agreed. When the Art Deco-styled terminal opened in May 1931, more than 50,000, some say 60,000, Tulsans turned out for the celebrations — the biggest convergence in Tulsa's history.

Pioneer Tulsans considered their water supply, the discolored, briney Arkansas River, undrinkable, in fact, not even fit for washing. Legend has it that a Tulsa bath was a three-part procedure: drawing the water and letting the silt settle, bathing, then dusting off. The alternative from 1909 on was home-delivered bottled water from Charles Page's Sand Springs Bottled Water Co. The sweet-flavored water was said to be "equally pleasing mixed with tea or bourbon." A two-inch pipeline ran from Sand Springs to a Tulsa bottling company on West Third Street. The springs, a favorite camping spot for Indians, gave the city of Sand Springs its name.

Oilman and Sand Springs founder Charles Page, already successfully involved in the bottled water business that supplied thirsty Tulsa with drinkable water, built Shell Creek dam and reservoir to ensure an adequate water supply for Sand Springs. He wanted Tulsa to commit to the new water supply, but proponents of Spavinaw Reservoir won out.

They said it couldn't be done. Critics scoffed at a plan to bring water to Tulsa, entirely by gravity flow, from Spavinaw more than 60 miles away. Consultants who said it could be accomplished included George Goethals, supervising engineer for the Panama Canal.

Below, A train carrying 60-inch concrete pipe to Spavinaw.
Right, Laying pipe for Spavinaw water, May 1923.
Lower right, Raising steel molds, May 1923.
Lower left, The $7.5 million Spavinaw project was considered one of the engineering marvels of the day and was, at the time, the third largest water project in the U.S.

Sweet, clear water replaced Arkansas brine at Tulsa taps when the gates of Spavinaw opened in the fall of 1924.

Built in 1916 as a two-lane span and widened to four lanes in 1935, the 11th Street Bridge once was part of U.S. 66, the famed link between Chicago and the West Coast. The span, located on Tulsa's most historic bridge site, originally was a pedestrian-wagon toll bridge. It was built in 1903 with a private "stud-horse note" and assured the city's access to just-discovered oil fields.

Despite the Depression, Tulsa was spreading steadily southward and needed another bridge. Construction of the gracefully arched 21st Street Bridge began in 1931.

The Frisco Railroad Depot was Tulsa's historic front door, but increasingly heavy rail activity created traffic jams at railroad crossings as more automobiles filled the streets. The station was torn down to make way for the 1931 opening of the Union Depot complex that incorporated traffic-easing viaducts for downtown's major avenues.

The Tulsa Education Special toured eastern cities in 1926 touting Tulsa. A Tulsa skyline was painted on the side of the train and its cargo included a miniature working refinery as well as a printing press for publishing a daily newspaper.

Heralded as Tulsa's most magnificent improvement, the Union Depot, a $3.5 million project, opened May 12, 1931, to a crowd of 60,000. Highlighting the dedication was the steam-whistling arrival of the Frisco's "Old 94," the first passenger train to chug into pioneer Tulsa.

Red caps posed on the Union Depot's opening day.

The Union Depot cafe.

The main waiting room had a 32-foot ceiling illuminated by four extravagant lighting fixtures each with a spread of about five feet.

The newsstand offered papers from as far away as New York City.

"Ride Busses Everywhere. THEY'RE CONVENIENT" was the motto of the original Union Bus Station, Fourth Street and Cincinnati Avenue. An early-day bus, *below*, ready for boarding. *(Courtesy of HW Allen Co.)*

Oilman Waite Phillips decided Tulsa needed a first-class bus depot and converted the Columbia Hotel into the Union Bus Terminal. In the '30s, the Art Deco terminal was considered one of the finest in the country.

Below, A fleet of MK&O buses at the station. *(Courtesy HW Allen Co.)* *Lower left*, H.W. Allen, founder of MK&O Coach Lines, with one of his first buses. *(Courtesy HW Allen Co.)* *Lower right*, Inside the Union Bus Terminal.

In 1916, Maple Ridge was one of Tulsa's newest neighborhoods. *Right*, the J.B. Means residence, 1132 E. 18th St.

From atop St. John Hospital, a view of 19th Street and Utica Avenue in the '20s.

Looking southeast from St. John Hospital in the mid-'20s, 21st Street was in the foreground of farmland that would become Utica Square.

In the '20s, 15th Street at the M-K-T Railroad overpass was still spanking new.

Looking north on Riverside Drive from 31st Street in the late '20s.

Left, A roadside cafe in Turley in the late '20s.

Lower left, Whittier Square at Admiral Boulevard and Lewis Avenue was Tulsa's first shopping center. By the '30s, the square boasted everything a suburban family could need from grocery stores to dry cleaners to cafes. The Circle Theater was the first movie house to open away from downtown.

Below, A Safeway store in 1935 at Boston Avenue and 18th Street.

Barall Food Stores, 2308 E. Admiral Blvd., was a familiar fixture in Whittier Square in the '30s.

Inside Barall Food Stores.

The Mincks Poultry Farm at 21st Street and Lewis Avenue in 1928 boasted 1,200 chickens. The same family built the Mincks Hotel, which later became the Adams Hotel.

The Lou North residence at the southeast corner of 51st Street and Harvard Avenue about 1912.

Above left, The El Patio Hotel, in 1938, was across the street from St. John Hospital.

Above right, The Colonial Building and Inn, northeast corner of 15th Street and Quaker Avenue, in 1927.

Left, Looking east toward 15th Street and Lewis Avenue. To the right of 15th Street was the Gillette Mansion built in 1921 as a country retreat.

Nearby Sapulpa was born of a trading post and named in 1886 by railroaders who boarded with an Indian family, the Sapulpas. As with Tulsa, the discovery of oil brought growth. *Right*, Sapulpa in 1925.
Getting there: the Sapulpa & Interurban Railway Co., *below*.

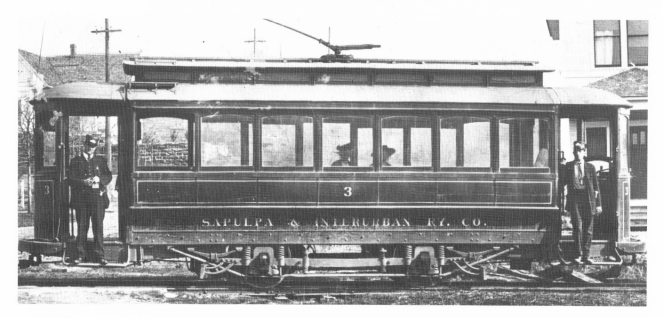

Rail service began in 1911 on the Sand Springs Interurban Railway. By 1923, the Interurban left Tulsa for Sand Springs every 20 minutes. In 1923 alone, the railway transported 3.7 million passengers.

The Sand Springs Interurban, about 1923, provided transportation for the Salvation Army's "annual free outing" for "1,200 poor Mothers and Kiddys."

Charles Page said he "bought the land to do good with" and built the Sand Springs Home, *above*, for orphans and widows and their children. Young residents, *right*, posed for a group photograph.

A Pierce Oil Corp. truck, *right*, about 1923, did double duty to transport high-school boosters campaigning for hard-surfaced roads.

Cotton wagons were a familiar sight on Main Street, Sand Springs, *left*, in 1918. Charles Page, one of Oklahoma's wealthiest oilmen who built what was called the largest textile mill west of the Mississippi River, posed with his cotton crews. *Lower left*, Main Street about two decades later.

Above, Nu-Flake Cereal Co. was touted as the "first and only breakfast food made in the Southwest." Operated by the Sand Springs Home, it was one of the town's first employers.

91

From the first, Tulsans had a love affair with the air.

THE SKY'S THE LIMIT

Tulsa's progress pivoted on the stud-horse note, money provided by gutsy and foresighted entrepreneurs to finance what would become vital civic improvements.

When voters said "no," it was a private stud-horse note in 1903 that built the 11th Street Bridge. The historic span assured Tulsa's prominence in the oil business by providing a reliable way to move workers and equipment across the Arkansas River to the Red Fork and Glenn Pool oil fields.

In 1928, the stud-horse note sent the city flying high into what would be a vital new industry: aviation.

Auto magnate Henry Ford, looking skyward, wanted passenger travel via his new Tri-Motor airships to be as routine as taking a spin in one of his omnipresent flivvers.

To promote the airways, he launched a city-to-city flying circus, the Ford Reliability Tour. Tulsa was told that it could be a 1928 tour stop — if, in six months, it could put together an airport capable of handling 50 airplanes.

Tulsa already had McIntyre Airport, founded in 1919 by former Air Force instructor Duncan McIntyre, dubbed the "Father of Tulsa Aviation." McIntyre was the site of the historic Sept. 30, 1927, gathering of eagles, the meeting of Charles Lindbergh and Arthur Goebel. The field accommodated thousands of cheering spectators but was too small for Ford's extravaganza.

With no time to go to the polls, 47 wealthy businessmen, led by oilman W.G. Skelly, signed a stud-horse note for $172,000 to purchase a 390-acre tract of land at the northeast corner of Sheridan Road and Apache Street. A wheat field was mowed into two runways and a tarpaper-roofed terminal, resembling an elongated cow barn, was thrown up within a week. But by July 3, 1928, Tulsa Municipal Airport was ready to host a legion of winged representatives of America's fledgling aviation industry.

The hoopla lasted three days, but when it ended, Tulsa was hooked on the air age.

By year's end, the airport had its first brick and steel hangar. What's more, Skelly, now even more of an aviation enthusiast, founded Spartan Aircraft Co. and Spartan School of Aeronautics that same year. In February 1929, with fellow oil cronies, he began S.A.F.E. Way Air Lines with Ford Tri-Motors and service between Kansas City, St. Louis, Tulsa, Fort Worth and Dallas.

By 1930, it was a time for bragging. And that's exactly what Charles W. Short, the airport's legendary manager, did. On an outdoor bulletin board, he began posting airport statistics, and declared Tulsa Municipal "busier" than even London's famed Croyden Airport. Would the truth be known, some airport insiders said later, Short's tally also included every landing and takeoff of Spartan students, spectators, meter readers, taxi drivers and the postman. But no matter. Tulsa had earned her wings.

Local aviation history was made on Sept. 30, 1927, when Charles Lindbergh, fresh from his non-stop flight across the Atlantic Ocean, landed the "Spirit of St. Louis" at Tulsa's McIntyre Airport. Tulsa dubbed the occasion "Lindbergh Day." Schools were closed and thousands turned out to cheer.

Another aviator, Arthur Goebel, who had piloted his "Woolaroc" non-stop across the Pacific Ocean to Hawaii, flew to Tulsa to greet Lindbergh, *seated in the plane.* Lindbergh, *second from left,* and Goebel, *right,* posed with Tulsa Mayor H.L. Newblock, *center.* Before Lindbergh agreed to visit, he established rules to protect himself from wellwishers. He objected "to being poked, punched or slapped on the back."

94

Arthur Goebel's golden-winged "Woolaroc" at Tulsa's McIntyre Airport. The Travel Air plane was sponsored by Phillips Petroleum Co. of Bartlesville.

Dubbed the "Father of Tulsa Aviation," Duncan A. McIntyre came to town in 1919, rented acreage at the southeast corner of Apache Street and Sheridan Road and called it an airport. By 1922, he was offering sightseeing tours over the city for $20 and round trips to Houston for $400. Later, he bought a site for his airport at Admiral Place and Sheridan Road, *above*, and provided the runways for the Lindbergh and Goebel landings. *Left*, McIntyre and a passenger preparing to take off.

95

Posing at Tulsa Municipal Airport was W.G. Skelly, *fourth from left*, one of Tulsa's premier oil barons who assured Tulsa's place in the fledgling aviation age. To left of Skelly is Will Rogers. At far right is Charles W. Short, Tulsa's first airport manager and for 30 years the city's unofficial "greeter" of the famous.

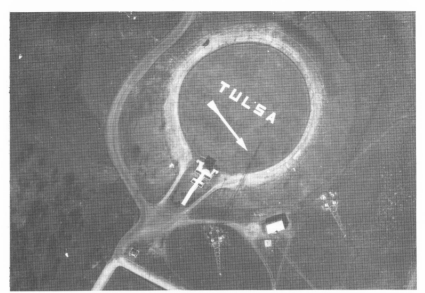

Atop Reservoir Hill, a 157-long sign outlined in white crushed stone pointed early aviators to Tulsa Municipal and McIntyre airports.

The original Tulsa Municipal Airport, a former wheat field, was financed in 1928 with a "stud-horse note" signed by almost 50 Tulsa businessmen. The crude terminal was said to have been erected in a week to be ready for Henry Ford's "Reliability Tour" of 25 to 50 planes to promote his Ford Tri-Motor for safe passenger travel. A winged arch served as gateway to the airport, *right*.

The first air-
plane built in
Tulsa, with de-
signer Willis C.
Brown, *right*,
and builder Paul
Meng. Tulsa
was said to have
major potential
for airplane
manufacturing
because of not
only its central
location but also
a fairly constant
humidity. Wood
was a major
component of
planes and hu-
midity changes
m a d e wings
come apart or
warp.

The first air mail service to Tulsa coincided with the opening of the
Municipal Airport in 1928.

It wasn't uncommon for local oil companies to have their own
airplanes. Barnsdall Corp. takes to the air in 1928.

A crowd greeted Wiley Post, renowned for his record-making flights, as he descended from his plane. Suited up to fly in the pressure uniform he designed for high altitudes, Post posed with oil baron Frank Phillips. Post died in the same 1935 Alaskan air crash that killed Will Rogers.

J.A. Woodring at McIntyre
Airport in 1925.

Picnics and straw hats had a place in early airport
activities when planes still rested on grass.

Aircraft on the ground and off at Tulsa Municipal
Airport.

An early-day ground crew.

Dorothy McBirney taking to the Tulsa
skies.

100

A U.S. Army C-71 blimp was tethered next to a hangar at Tulsa Municipal Airport about 1929.

W.G. Skelly not only led the "stud-horse note" campaign that financed Tulsa's airport, but also went two steps further to assure Tulsa's reputation in the air. He built Spartan Aircraft Co. and the Spartan School of Aeronautics.

A lineup of Spartan training planes.

Spartan first produced the "Executive," a private, luxury airplane, in 1935. This experimental craft was the prototype.

Crew and mechanics posed in a Tulsa hangar with a S.A.F.E Way Airlines Tri-Motor. W.G. Skelly and other oil-wealthy Tulsans founded the line in 1929. The planes carried 14 and first service was between Kansas City, St. Louis, Tulsa, Fort Worth and Dallas.

Bands paraded, dignitaries gathered and crowds poured in
when Tulsa dedicated a new air terminal in 1932.

104

Tulsa's new Municipal Airport, with Spartan School of Aeronautics in the left background. The terminal's waiting area featured the era's popular Art Deco styling.

Making way for the trolley, a construction crew paved the Third Street Bridge in 1924.

A TIME TO WORK

Tulsa's first workers were primarily shopkeepers who supplied the basics to engineers and track layers who brought the railroad to town.

Then, in 1905, Glenn Pool was discovered, oil fever struck and the city's labor force rapidly reassembled around black gold. Not only were there jobs in the oil fields and refineries, but also in countless support fields ranging from derrick manufacturing to clerking in banks that catered to oilmen.

By 1928, the city boasted an output of more than $64 million in petroleum products, $9 million in derricks, rigs and tanks, plus another $5 million in other oil-field supplies.

It was oil that lured Tulsa's job force. At the century's turn, the city's population was little more than 1,000. By 1920, it was 72,000; by 1930, 142,000. Between 1920 and 1930, Tulsa jumped from 100th in size among American cities to 49th.

Although it was the gush of oil prosperity that primarily drew job seekers, Tulsa's prime industry was far from the only source of a paycheck.

In 1928, for example, Tulsa's "entire industrial output" was reckoned at $113 million, thanks to a variety of industries, including foundries, glass manufacturers, printing, lumber, cotton mills, and brick and tile. The same year, the opening of Tulsa's Municipal Airport as well as Spartan School of Aeronautics and Spartan Aircraft Co. began providing a new source of employment: aviation. It would become one of Tulsa's biggest employers.

The city's tremendous growth kept Tulsans on the job. In the one-time dusty cow town, there were streets to be paved, sewers to be dug and bridges to be built. Skyscrapers were a constant source of employment. The city was so entranced with growth that substantial masonry structures sometimes claimed a downtown corner for only a few years before being leveled for buildings that were bigger and better.

Even during the Depression, many Tulsans kept working, thanks to ambitious building projects that refused to bow to the hard times. The Union Depot, the new municipal airport, additions to the federal building and the Philcade building proved a boon to hundreds during that worst of times.

The horses that pulled Tulsa's early fire wagons were sold to Kansas City in 1913 when the Tulsa department switched to the gasoline engine for its horsepower.

Fully mechanized, Tulsa fire fighters showed off their new equipment in 1914 at the southwest corner of Third Street and Boulder Avenue.

Firemen battled freezing weather and flames on Dec. 10, 1919, when Garner Drug Store, on the west side of Main Street near Second Street, went up in smoke.

Municipal improvements in 1912 included new sewer lines.

Workers surfaced the Third Street Bridge in 1924.

111

U.S. Deputy Marshal John Moran leading a liquor raid in 1915.

112

Down the drain went hundreds of bottles of confiscated hooch under the supervision of U.S. Deputy Marshal John Moran.

Above, A spittoon received prominant placement in 1916 at the U.S. marshals' office in the Cole Building, northwest corner of Fifth Street and Boston Avenue.

Above right, U.S. Deputy Marshal John Moran at the wheel in 1921, making Christmas deliveries.

Right, Tulsa police mustered for duty in 1912.

Automobiles were overhauled at Carter Oil Co.'s repair shop, 820 N. Lewis Ave.

Dust hoods and side curtains
were big sellers in 1917 at the
Modern Auto Shop, 405 S.
Frankfort Ave. Owner George
Green posed in his office.

116

The K.C. Auto Hotel, 313 S. Cincinnati Ave., did a brisk business with rental cars and trucks about 1930. Parking was 35 cents for four hours, 50 cents for 12 hours.

Below, The first "big truck" used by Shannon's Furniture, Second and Main streets, about 1925.

The Economy Tire Co., 7 E. Seventh St., in 1918 boasted "the most trustworthy tires built."

At Tulsa Shoe Rebuilders, 405 S. Boulder Ave., free pick-up and delivery was all part of the service.

Fresh produce found its way to Tulsa through the open-air Farmers' Market on North Trenton Avenue.

The Three-Point-Two Service Co., 1301 S. Cincinnati Ave., believed to be Tulsa's first beer franchise following Prohibition in 1933, advertised home delivery.

The Union Transportation Co.'s full fleet was on display in 1931 at the company's bus barn, Brady Street and Guthrie Avenue.

A Tulsa Street Railways Co. car in 1920 with the trolley interior and employees.

Employees of The Right Way Laundry, 210-212 S. Cincinnati Ave., went all out for a group photograph on March 30, 1923.

Laundry & Employees
1923 — TULSA OKLA

photo by Hoefler Shuler Photo Co. Inc.
TULSA OKLA

In 1919, the Guaranty Laundry not only washed your clothes but also delivered. The truck was parked in front of the Hasty Messenger Service, 107 W. Second St.

Peoples Ice Co., 205 W. First St., delivered the goods first by horse, then "electric ice wagon" and, ultimately, a fleet of ice trucks.

Carrying a 300-pound block of ice was all in a day's work for Peoples Ice Co. delivery man James W. Wilkerson Sr.

An indispensable household item was the ice card displayed outside to let delivery men know what size block to leave.

A young Beryl Ford used his bicycle to peddle popsicles in 1938.

Early fast food: The One Minute Lunch Room.

Oklahoma Dairy Co., in 1926. It later became Meadow Gold Dairy Products.

Women sewed buttons on fur coats in 1937 for Vandevers, which began as a pioneer dry-goods store and prospered to become one of Tulsa's leading department stores.

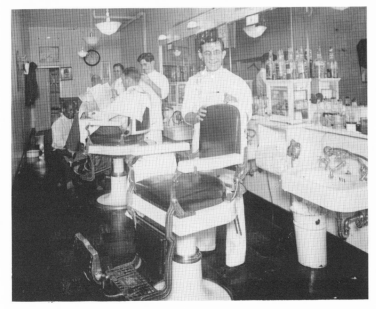

Barber Charley Hall waiting for a customer at the Guy Scott Barber Shop on West Fourth Street.

The Tulsa Undertaking Co. at Third Street and Xanthus Avenue in 1940. Inside were "slumber beds" where bodies rested before being placed in caskets.

Scenes of early
OTASCO stores.

Depression-bowed but still proud Tulsans found work on a WPA project constructing Recreation Lake at Mohawk Park. *(Courtesy of Hugh S. Davis.)*

BAD TIMES

Tulsa was a star-kissed city, but there were bad times, both man-made and at nature's whim.

In 1921, Tulsa was the scene of one of America's most devastating race riots.

The war was sparked by an encounter between a black bootblack and a white female elevator operator in a downtown office building. The bootblack was arrested, rumors of a lynching spread and angry mobs of blacks and whites gathered at the jail. The white gang marched on black North Tulsa, shooting, looting and burning. The National Guard was called in and, according to a newspaper account, "twenty minutes of withering machine gun fire ended the battle." North Tulsa, it concluded, resembled "the ruins of a town hit simultaneously by fire and tornado."

What really happened on that downtown elevator? How many Tulsans were slain? No one knew for sure. It was the city's darkest hour.

West Tulsa bore the brunt of nature's riotousness in June 1923 when the Arkansas River roiled over its banks with flood waters that would not be bested for decades. Four thousand Tulsans were left homeless, refineries were flooded and power and water supplies were knocked out. All roads leading to the city, except from the north, were closed. Travel between Tulsa and Sand Springs was strictly by boat.

The '20s was a time of extraordinary prosperity for most of Tulsa. Thanks to that "flywheel economy," the city was one of the last to be bowed by the Depression. Eventually, however, the oil industry was hit, and by the winter of 1931, Tulsa had soup lines, beggars at doorsteps and "We Want Work" parades. Hungry families, desperate for work, camped on the courthouse steps. Plums were city project jobs that paid $3 per day for a three-day work week.

By 1932, 7,000 Tulsans were jobless. In December 1932, 130 unemployed men marched eight miles through six-inch snow for a timber-cutting job on Bird Creek.

Help for the jobless came from the federal Works Progress Administration. WPA projects, 27 in the Tulsa area, were dubbed "make work" but provided Tulsa with major improvements including a new reservoir at Mohawk Park and the Tulsa Rose Garden.

The Depression cost jobs and, in the process, set the scene for labor unrest. In December 1938, Tulsa was center stage when Mid-Continent Petroleum Corp. was struck by its West Tulsa refinery workers.

The conflict, which lasted until March 1940, was bitter, with National Guardsmen called in to protect the refinery with bayonets, machine guns and barbed-wire barriers. The strike made nationwide headlines as a precedent-setting labor dispute. It also became a Tulsa sightseeing attraction, causing daily traffic jams as motorists gawked at the refinery-turned-armed-camp.

On May 31, 1921, threats of a lynching, a black march to the city jail and an angry, arsonist white mob combined to trigger two days of fighting that left 35 blocks of North Tulsa burned to the ground.

132

133

Victims sift through the riot's rubble as tents serve as makeshift shelters. Reports placed the destruction toll at 800 buildings with many families losing all their belongings.

135

Mt. Zion Baptist Church, *far left*, which cost Tulsa's black community $85,000, was reduced to a smouldering hulk in the riot only six weeks after it was completed. Some reports indicated ammunition had been stored in the church.

137

Reconstruction in North Tulsa was a slow and painful process. Most families did not carry insurance. For those who did, the policies did not cover riot damage.

139

A sky blackened with smoke covered the devastation of North Tulsa on June 1, 1921.

Following the rioting, black Tulsans were herded by the National Guard to McNulty Park, 11th Street and Elgin Avenue.

White Tulsans gathered at Convention Hall as rumors and racial tensions mounted.

The National Guard was called in to quell the riot.

Ark. River at Tulsa
6-13-23

An entire train was parked as a giant weight on the Frisco Railroad bridge in June 1923 to prevent the bridge from washing away with record Arkansas River flood waters.

Flood waters in 1923 washed through homes north of Sand Springs Road near 33rd West Avenue, *above*, and in the vicinity of Home Gardens on the Sand Springs line, *left*.

143

Depression-era jobless Tulsans in 1934 made a living turning a gulch into the Tulsa Rose Garden, 1370 E. 24th Place. (*Courtesy of Hugh S. Davis.*)

A WPA project transformed a trash- and weed-strewn gully between the George Snedden Mansion and Woodward Park into a world-famous rose garden. Work was done primarily by hand and horse teams to provide as many jobs as possible. *Above*, the $750,000 finished product. The Snedden Mansion, *left of the garden*, became the Tulsa Garden Center. (*Courtesy of Hugh S. Davis.*)

The construction of Recreation Lake in Mohawk Park was another federal "make work" project. (*Courtesy of Hugh S. Davis.*)

Pick, shovel and sweat of the brow provided most of the horsepower for Recreation Lake construction. *Left*, the finished product. (*Courtesy of Hugh S. Davis.*)

147

Above, Tracy Park, 11th Street and Peoria Avenue, boasted tennis courts in the '30s, thanks to the WPA. (*Courtesy of Hugh S. Davis.*)

Right, WPA workers were mustered at Newblock Park before being trucked to work sites. (*Courtesy of Hugh S. Davis.*)

148

Originally built by the "Prince of Petroleum," Josh Cosden, the Mid-Continent refinery in West Tulsa was the site of a violent strike that began at Christmastime 1938 and would not be settled until March 1940. Pickets, who would be driven away by police with tear gas, gathered at the refinery gates.

Striking union men prevented a truck loaded with ice from entering the refinery.

National Guard troops were stationed around the refinery. Col. Charles A. Holden, commander of the strike-duty troops, ordered pickets to disperse.

National Guardsmen practiced with bayonets in the "military zone" surrounding the Mid-Continent refinery. *Inset*, a solider standing guard at the barbed-wire entanglements set up along the Arkansas River bank near the 11th Street Bridge.

151

The Salvation Army String Band tuning up in the early '30s.

COMMUNITY TIES

The gush of oil injected Tulsa with a gush of prosperity, but often unrefined. Taming the boom town into a community meant tending to the mind, spirit and body of its citizens. Tulsans, often led by oilmen, rose to the occasion.

Churches were on the move. The city's pioneer sanctuaries were modest structures with windows routinely shot out by drunken cowpokes. But Tulsans' church-going nature endured, and their houses of worship became grander, climaxed by the 1929 completion of the modernistic Boston Avenue Methodist Church.

At the same time that oil millionaires were erecting mansions, tent cities still were pitched on the city's fringes. Hundreds of families, lured by the oil boom, were destitute. What's more, recreation for youth, rich and poor, was nil. The Arkansas River and hazardous coal pits were the only early swimming holes.

Often, it was at church meetings that these social problems first were tackled. Such a gathering of concerned businessmen gave rise to the Tulsa YMCA in 1909, a program so successful that it became known as the "Tulsa Plan" and was copied nationwide. A similar church gathering kicked off a 1913 fund-raising effort for the YMCA's first permanent headquarters.

Two hundred oilmen and other business leaders said that they would raise $100,000 in 10 days. On the eighth day, Thanksgiving Day, they had $122,000. The campaign, Tulsa's first communi-ty-wide, fund-raising project, became the proto-type for future community fund drives.

One outgrowth of the "Y" was the arrival of the Boy Scouts in 1911. A year later, Tulsa had the largest scout organization in the state.

Girl Scouting came to town in 1917 with Sunflower Troop No. 1. Early scouting activities included helping Arkansas River flood victims by collecting donated furniture and stitching up new gingham dresses for the homeless.

Tuberculosis became a health threat and Tulsans responded in 1918 with the free Anti-Tuberculosis Clinic. In 1924, it expanded into the Public Health Association. There were visiting nurses, free clinics, free cod liver oil and layettes and lots of good advice, including the advantages of giving birth in a hospital rather than at home.

That wasn't always the case.

At the turn of the century, when a Tulsan needed an appendix — or bullet — removed, the Frisco Depot was closed and doctors performed the surgery there.

By the late '20s, however, Tulsa boasted two fully equipped, modern hospitals: Morningside, now Hillcrest Medical Center, and what is today St. John Medical Center. What's more, the city in 1929 become a mecca for medical treatment in northeast Oklahoma as a result of the opening of the downtown Medical Arts Building.

A winning Girl Scouts' sales team in the early '30s.

154

Girl Scouting was in full swing in Tulsa in the early '30s. Bus field trips and parades were popular activities.

Tulsa's Boy Scout Troop No. 1 in the '30s.

Tulsa's newest citizens posed with their mothers at the Public Health Association, 724 S. Elgin Ave., in 1932. Organized in 1918, the agency provided weekly clinics for tuberculosis, child welfare, prenatal care and immunizations.

In the '20s and '30s, the Public Health Association was the only health service in Tulsa County to offer visiting nurses for the sick and needy. The agency's credo was that prevention was as important as the cure.

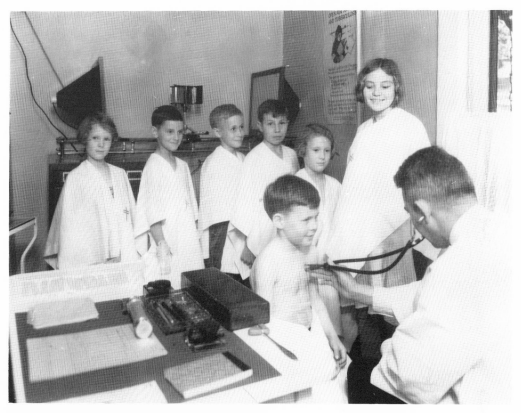

The Public Health Association had its beginnings as the Tulsa County Anti-Tuberculosis Society when TB was the nation's No. 1 killer. Children were routinely examined and participated in education efforts. Their slogan was: "From Whom did he get it? To Whom did he give it? Examine and Protect Every Contact."

159

Tulsans turned out in force with floats and flags on Sept. 14, 1915, at the ball park at Archer Street and Cincinnati Avenue. The occasion was what Tulsans dubbed a "durbar," a celebration of civic and fraternal clubs.

Opposite page, Boys heading off to summer camp in 1927 gathered in front of Tulsa's first YMCA on the northwest corner of Fourth Street and Cincinnati Avenue. The building, dedicated in 1914, had Tulsa's first indoor swimming pool.

FRATERNAL SOCIETIES
OKLAHOMA DURBAR
TULSA SEPT. 14-15.

CENTRAL HIGH SCHOOL, TULSA, OKLA.

Tulsa's first yellow brick high school was built in 1906 on the site of the Presbyterian Mission School, the city's first schoolhouse, Fourth Street and Boston Avenue.

In 1916, some students were turned away from Tulsa's high school because of overcrowding. The problem was solved a year later when the new Central High School, *left*, Sixth Street between Cincinnati and Detroit avenues, opened. Only five years later, Central High School expanded with a new south wing, *below*.

Kendall College, which opened its doors in Muskogee in 1894, established a permanent campus, *right*, in Tulsa in 1908. In 1921, Kendall College was officially chartered as the University of Tulsa with a record freshman enrollment of 60 students.

In 1930, the University of Tulsa dominated the surrounding landscape. Skelly Stadium, *right*, funded by W.G. Skelly and other citizens, was under construction.

Will Rogers High School, 3909 E. Fifth Place, *below*, opened Sept. 11, 1939, and was quickly nicknamed "Will on the Hill." Prairie-like open space surrounded the school that students, warned to beware of grazing cattle, reached by cow path from 11th Street. *Right*, Will Rogers posed with his aunts in 1926.

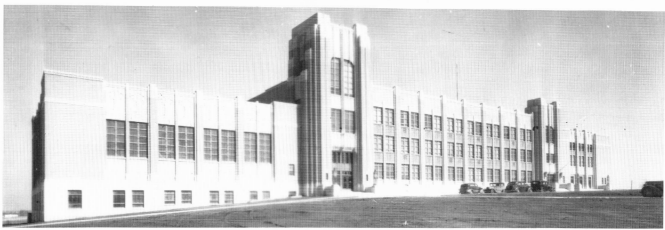

Top left, Holy Family Cathedral, at Eighth Street and Boulder Avenue, in 1927. *Left*, Excavating for the cathedral, which was dedicated in 1914.

Top right, Christian Church, southwest corner of Fourth Street and Boulder Avenue, in 1912.

Lower right, First Christian Church, Ninth Street and Boulder Avenue, was organized in 1902.

167

Above, First Baptist Church of Tulsa, Fourth Street and Cincinnati Avenue, shortly after completion in 1927.
Top right, First Presbyterian Church, Seventh Street and Boston Avenue, in 1926. *Right*, First Presbyterian Church in 1915, half the size and lacking a spire.

168

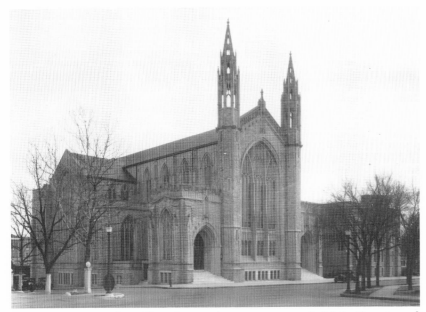

First Methodist Church, southeast corner of 11th Street and Boulder Avenue, in the early '20s.

First Church of Christian Science, northwest corner of 11th Street and Boulder Avenue, in 1926.

Called the first 20th Century Church, the modernistic Boston Avenue Methodist Church, *above*, was considered out in the suburbs when it was built at 13th Street and Boston Avenue in 1929. The congregation, in 1919, had much more modest quarters at Fifth Street and Boston Avenue, *left*.

169

Dedicated in 1928, Morningside Hospital, 1600 E. 12th St., *above*, was sold to Hillcrest Memorial Hospital in 1940. Its first location was 521 N. Boulder Ave.

The Medical Arts Building, southwest corner of Sixth Street and Boulder Avenue, was completed in 1929 and drew patients from all of northeastern Oklahoma. The idea for the building was conceived when doctors and dentists were being crowded out of office space because of increasing demands by the expanding oil companies.

St. John Hospital, 21st Street and Utica Avenue, was opened in 1926 by the Sisters of the Sorrowful Mother, who in 1918 paid $16,000 for an eight-acre site then considered out in the country. That first year, the sisters cared for 1,958 patients.

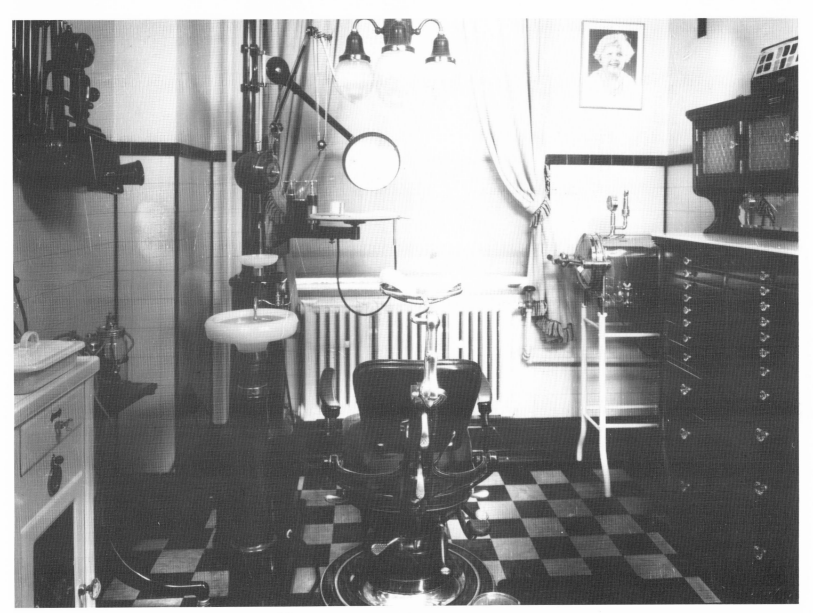

A dentist's office in the Medical Arts Building.

Young Lee McBirney setting off for a spin in his goat cart.

A TIME TO PLAY

Tulsans always have reveled in a good time, and from the beginnings of the oil boom, through the "fat" '20s, the Depression tragedies of the '30s and the devil-may-care era that ushered in World War II, downtown was the place to be.

Downtown was synonymous with grand old movie palaces. The Ritz. The Orpheum. The Majestic. The Rialto. At these elite theaters, not only were there ushers, but also "spielers," young men in uniform and swinging a baton, whose job it was to tell theatergoers how long before a seat would be open.

And an evening at the movies meant more than a movie. There was a concert by an orchestra or band, a newsreel and a cartoon, not to mention organ-accompanied sing-alongs. The theaters were shows in themselves. The Ritz, for example, took the theme of an Italian Renaissance palace, complete with life-size statuary and a ceiling studded with twinkling stars — and the illusion of drifting clouds. "The patron," waxed one newspaper reporter on opening night, "is transplanted from familiar streets to the languorous land of the blue Mediterranean."

Vaudeville was in its heyday in the '20s, and Tulsa got the cream of the crop. In 1924, the Orpheum headlined Mae West. Other top names included Jimmy Durante, Sally Rand, Eddie Cantor, George Jessel and Rudy Vallee. When the Akdar Theater swung wide its doors in 1925, it proclaimed itself "Oklahoma's Most Beautiful Playhouse" and treated its first-nighters to the Ziegfeld Broadway hit "Sally," featuring "75 beautiful and talented girls."

Not all of Tulsa's entertainment, however, was imported. In 1934, the city spotted itself on the entertainment map when Bob Wills and His Texas Playboys introduced the country to western swing, broadcast live on KVOO from Cain's Academy of Dancing.

Tulsa's premier downtown entertainment center, the Coliseum, opened New Year's Day 1929. Originally built as a showcase for ice hockey, the Coliseum housed events for every taste, from wrestling to piano competitions, ballroom dancing to political rallies, basketball games to high-school graduations.

The Coliseum ultimately burned. The majestic movie palaces were razed. Ironically, it was Convention Hall, today the Brady Steet Theater, that endured. Built in 1914, the hall hosted events ranging from the first International Petroleum Exposition to a performance by Italian tenor Enrico Caruso. Yet almost immediately, it was branded a white elephant. Its biggest problem, save the trains rumbling by less than a block away, was the stage which sloped 13 inches foward. That was great for audience viewing, its designers reasoned. But it was rough on unsuspecting performers, like an infuriated prima ballerina Mme. Pavlova, who could barely tiptoe up the incline, or a startled roller skater, who almost wheeled into the audience's lap.

173

A day at the races was a popular Tulsa pastime, and Eaton's Band entertained fans between runs at the Tulsa Fairgrounds' track, Lewis Avenue and Archer Street, in 1920.

Betting on horse racing was illegal in Oklahoma, but stakes still were high at the track at the old Tulsa Fairgrounds. To put a stop to the gambling, National Guardsmen from Stillwater were sent to the track in April 1914 to halt the races. Promoters, the story went, refused to comply until the guardsmen fired a volley of shots over the horses' heads.

Golf was a growing sport with a large following in Tulsa in the '20s.
Top, Tulsa Country Club in 1929.
Above and right, Highland Golf Course, 21st Street and Yale Avenue, where golfers putted on sand greens.

Tulsa Country Club attracted top golfers and important tournaments in the '20s.

Football at McNulty Park, 11th Street and Elgin Avenue, was played on a 90-yard field around 1920.

In 1916, the Kendall College football team was regarded as the best in the Southwest. Coached by Sam McBirney, *far left*, and Francis Schmidt, *far right*, Kendall outscored opponents, 566 to 50, while compiling a record of 10 victories without a loss. Included was a 117-0 decision over Missouri Mines.

178

W.G. Skelly was the chief contributor to the University of Tulsa's Skelly Stadium, built in 1930.

The jalopy, the more dilapidated the better, was the vehicle of choice at "junk car races" in the '30s near 21st Street and Yale Avenue at what would become Mayo Meadows.

Horse and rider plunged headlong into a water tank at the 1939 Tulsa State Fair.

When Tulsa hosted a rose carnival in 1926, seniors at Conway Broun School turned an automobile into a flower garden on wheels.

Tulsa old-timers, members of the Pioneer Association, gathered in about 1920 for a picnic at the Lon Stansbury summer home in Alsuma, southeast of Tulsa. A nostalgic replica of Tulsa's original downtown storefronts decorated Stansbury Lake. The lake was formed by the Davie Burnt Clay Ballast Co. that sold burnt clay to the Katy Railroad for its road bed in the early 1900s.

The Reed wading pool in Central Park, Sixth Street and Peoria Avenue, offered an attractive alternative to the ol' swimming hole.

182   Woodward Park, 21st Street and Peoria Avenue, shown here in the 'Teens, was purchased by the city of Tulsa for park land at $100 an acre in 1909 despite citizen protest that the land was "way out in the country" and accessible only by wagon trails.

Mohawk Park, once considered "Oklahoma's greatest recreational center," was a fortuitous offshoot of Tulsa's 1923 Spavinaw Dam project. Mohawk Reservoir was built to store water from Spavinaw and private citizens, realizing the park's potential, bought up surrounding acreage. The park was enhanced during the Depression with "make work" projects ranging from picnic tables to zoo facilities.

Crown Drug, southwest corner of Fourth and Main streets, drew a nattily attired crowd in the early '40s. Old King beer, "Oklahoma's Own," was 10 cents a bottle; a bacon-and-egg breakfast was 20 cents.

A downtown tradition for more than a half-century and center for the city's late-night life, Bishop's Restaurant, 521 S. Main St., was originally Bishop's Waffle House, *on left side of street*, located at Second Street and Boston Avenue, until about 1930.

Vandevers was the city's first "family," or department, store. In 1926, Vandevers outfitted Miss Tulsa, Norma Smallwood, who later was crowned Miss America. This was Vandevers, Fifth Street between Main Street and Boston Avenue, in 1932.

Seidenbach's, considered one of Tulsa's most exclusive women's stores, at 413 S. Main St. in the late '20s.

The Hunt Building, southeast corner of Fourth and Main streets, in the '20s became headquarters for Brown-Dunkin, once one of the largest department stores in the Southwest.

Palace Clothiers, a fashionable men's store, on the northwest corner of Fourth and Main streets, in the '20s.

Sears moved to the southwest corner of Fifth Street and Boulder Avenue, *above*, in 1931 from a smaller location at 624 S. Boston Ave.

Christmastime in downtown Tulsa in the '30s and '40s found Main Street festooned with real evergreen garlands and trees asparkle at night.

The Akdar Theater, *right*, built at Fourth Street and Denver Avenue at the peak of the oil building boom, was a mosque for the Akdar Shrine, but also proclaimed itself "Oklahoma's Most Beautiful Playhouse." A Ziegfeld Broadway musical production, "Sally," opened the theater.

A tent at Delaware Avenue and 15th Street was the 1928 site of Tulsa Little Theatre.

Conventions meant growth, but booming Tulsa had no large public facility. The solution was Convention Hall, built in 1914 at Brady Street and Boulder Avenue. With seating for 4,200, it was considered, at the time, the largest and best public auditorium between Kansas City and Houston. It housed events ranging from the first International Petroleum Exposition in 1923 to performances by Italian tenor Enrico Caruso and prima ballerina Anna Pavlova.

188

It was a figurative cast of thousands when the University of Tulsa presented "Aida" at Skelly Stadium in July 1933.

The Coliseum, southeast corner of Fifth Street and Elgin Avenue, opened New Year's Day 1929 and became Tulsa's entertainment center and sports palace. The city's largest auditorium was built to showcase hockey, but it provided a stage for events ranging from musical recitals to wrestling matches that raised money for the Babies Free Milk Fund. Opening day reportedly featured the first professional hockey game south of the Mason-Dixon Line.

As versatile as it was elegant, the Coliseum was host to state political conventions as well as the Ice Follies.

191

Piano competitions and the D-X Diamond Oilers, the 1933 Amateur Athletic Union's national championship basketball team, took center stage at the Coliseum.

The Orpheum, on Fourth Street between Main Street and Boston Avenue, opened in 1924 as a vaudeville theater where the likes of Mae West, Sally Rand and Jimmy Durante performed. Movies were not shown until 1929.

The Majestic Theater, built in 1918 at 406 S. Main St., boasted the largest marquee in Oklahoma. Until the Ritz was built, it reigned supreme among Tulsa's movie theaters and reportedly was the first Tulsa theater to show a sound movie. In 1941, when "Shepherd of the Hills," starring John Wayne, made its premiere, the crowd started lining up at 6 a.m., five hours before the first show.

When Tulsa was a theater town: the Orpheum advertised "high class vaudeville and photoplays," the Rialto presented "high class feature photoplays and stage presentations," and the Main Street offered "first run Western photoplays."

The Grand Promenade, Mezzanine floor, of the Ritz.

The Ritz, 18 W. Fourth St., opened in May 1926 and became Tulsa's premier theater. Its Italian Renaissance-style decor, including life-size statues and a ceiling of twinkling stars, prompted one reporter to write of opening night: "As if by magic, the patron is transplanted from familiar streets to the languorous land of the blue Mediterranean."

Cain's, built in 1924 as a garage at 423 N. Main St., became Cain's Academy of Dancing in 1930. It was here that Bob Wills and his band, the Texas Playboys, in 1935 popularized the music form called western swing. At one mid-'30s session, the band consisted of, *from left*, Eldon Shamblin, Son Lansford, Bob Wills, Johnnie Lee Wills, Tommy Duncan and Leon McAuliffe.

While based in Tulsa in the '30s and early '40s, Bob Wills and His Texas Playboys frequently traveled by bus to out-of-town engagements. In 1934, about a month after their arrival in Tulsa, the Playboys consisted of, *from left*, O.W. Mayo, Son Lansford, Everett Stover, Johnnie Lee Wills, June Whalin, Bob Wills, Tommy Duncan and Kermit Whalin.

In 1926, 18-year-old Miss Tulsa Norma Smallwood was crowned Miss America. Two years later, while a headliner on a vaudeville circuit, she met and married Tulsa oilman Thomas Gilcrease. They were divorced in 1934.

Bob Wills, known almost as much for his cowboy hat as for his music, drew crowds not only at Cain's for dancing but also on Main Street for the parades that heralded the arrival of his annual Bob Wills Tulsa Stampede Rodeo.

Tulsa's patriotic efforts in the early days of World War II included home-front parades by Civil Defense workers, including neighborhood wardens. Marchers heading south on Boston Avenue.

WINDS OF WAR

During World War I, Tulsa's patriotic efforts were an example to the nation. The outbreak of World War II triggered the same response.

Tulsans again were rolling Red Cross bandages, buying war bonds in record amounts and staging spirited downtown parades.

What's more, the city that fueled the country's first war effort with increased oil production had a new vital industry to offer: aviation.

Even before the United States entered the war, Spartan School of Aeronautics, founded by aviation enthusiast W.G. Skelly, was training flyers for the Allies. Ultimately, more than 20,000 pilots got their wings in Tulsa during World War II. Some 5,000 war-time mechanics also were trained at Spartan.

Spartan Aircraft Co. quickly began turning out aircraft assemblies for the war effort. But Spartan was far from the only Tulsa company that would keep the Allies flying. The city's oil-related businesses — foundaries, machine shops, metal-working plants — were ideally suited for turning out equipment needed for the combat effort. War contracts poured in and Tulsans found themselves assembling everything from gun barrels to parts for bomb sights and winches for landing craft.

Oklahoma, which ranked 33rd among states in pre-war manufacturing, jumped to 18th in war supply and facility contracts. More than 140 Tulsa firms engaged in major war-production manufacturing.

It was Skelly, too, who assured Tulsa's most prominent contribution to the war effort and boon to its own Depression-dulled economy: the Douglas Aircraft Co. bomber assembly plant. In 1941, when Skelly learned of President Franklin D. Roosevelt's plan to build thousands of airplanes a year to fight the war, he was off to Washington to convince the War Department that the bomber plant should be in Tulsa. The department agreed — if the city would provide the land. Less than two months later, Tulsans voted "yes," and construction of the $15 million Air Force Plant No. 3 began.

The plant, a mile long and windowless, transformed hundreds of housewives into "Rosie the Riveter," ready and willing to work 'round-the-clock to turn out the gleaming bombers that soared worldwide but were stamped "Made in Tulsa."

Instructors at Spartan School of Aeronautics, *above*, trained more than 20,000 pilots during World War II. Tulsa's Harvey Young Airport, *right*, served as a training center for the overflow.

Rookie pilots at Harvey Young Airport waiting for airborne action.

U.S.S. TULSA

Because of its liberty bond campaign in World War I, Tulsa in 1918 became the namesake of the unusual gun boat USS Tulsa, which sported masts and a steam engine. The vessel, later nicknamed the "Galloping Ghost Off the China Coast," was a spy ship against the Japanese in World War II.

A U.S. zeppelin glided over downtown Tulsa in 1929 as small planes provided an escort.

Just as in World War I, Tulsans were enthusiastic about buying war stamps and turning out for patriotic demonstrations.

Main Street took on an almost festive air when a replica of a railroad car rolled into town promising patriotic entertainment, American Legion fireworks and Sears-donated "orange juice for War Mothers."

Tulsans queued up for a city block in 1942 when a $1-million war bond drive shared the marquee with "Mrs. Miniver" at the Ritz Theater.

Inside the Ritz, every seat was filled and patriotism took center stage when the colors were paraded down the aisle.

PHOTO COLLAGE BY DAVE CARMAN